Seeing The World With One Eye

Acknowledgments: Several of these poems were previously published in *Adze, The Antigonish Review, The Cormorant, Event, The Fiddlehead, Germination, The Pottersfield Portfolio, Prairie Fire, Danger Falling Ice*, Joe Blades, ed. (BS Poetry Society), *Strong Winds*, Sheila Hyland, ed. (Broken Jaw Press), and Ghazals I to XXIV appeared in *The Slow Curve of the Past*, by Edward Gates, No. 14 in the Salamanca Chapbook Series (Wild East Publishing Co-operative Ltd.), Fredericton, NB.

Ghazals XVII, XXX, XXXI, XXXIV and XXXIX won First Prize (poetry) in the Writers' Federation of New Brunswick's 1990 Literary Competition.

Cover art by Dorena Gates
Data entry by Butterfly Irie Rowan
Design and in-house editing by Joe Blades
Printed and bound in Canada by Sentinel Printing, Yarmouth

The Author acknowledges the support of the Canada Council for the Arts-Explorations Program while writing some of these poems.

THE CANADA COUNCIL | LE CONSEIL DES ARTS
FOR THE ARTS | DU CANADA
SINCE 1957 | DEPUIS 1957

The Publisher acknowledges the support of the Canada Council for the Arts and the New Brunswick Department of Economic Development, Tourism and Culture-Arts Development Branch.

Canadian Cataloguing in Publication Data
Gates, Edward, 1950-

Seeing the world with one eye.

Poems.
ISBN 0-921411-69-3

I. Title.

PS8563.A784S44 1998   C811'.54   C98-950083-7
PR9199.3.G3734S44 1998

Broken Jaw Press
MARITIMES ARTS PROJECTS PRODUCTIONS
Box 596 Stn A
Fredericton NB E3B 5A6   ph/fax 506 454-5127
Canada   e-mail: jblades@nbnet.nb.ca

Seeing The World
With One Eye

Edward Gates

Fredericton • Canada

This book is dedicated to
Micheal Brian Oliver, Robert Hawkes,
Allan Cooper, Thomas Smith and Joe Blades

I

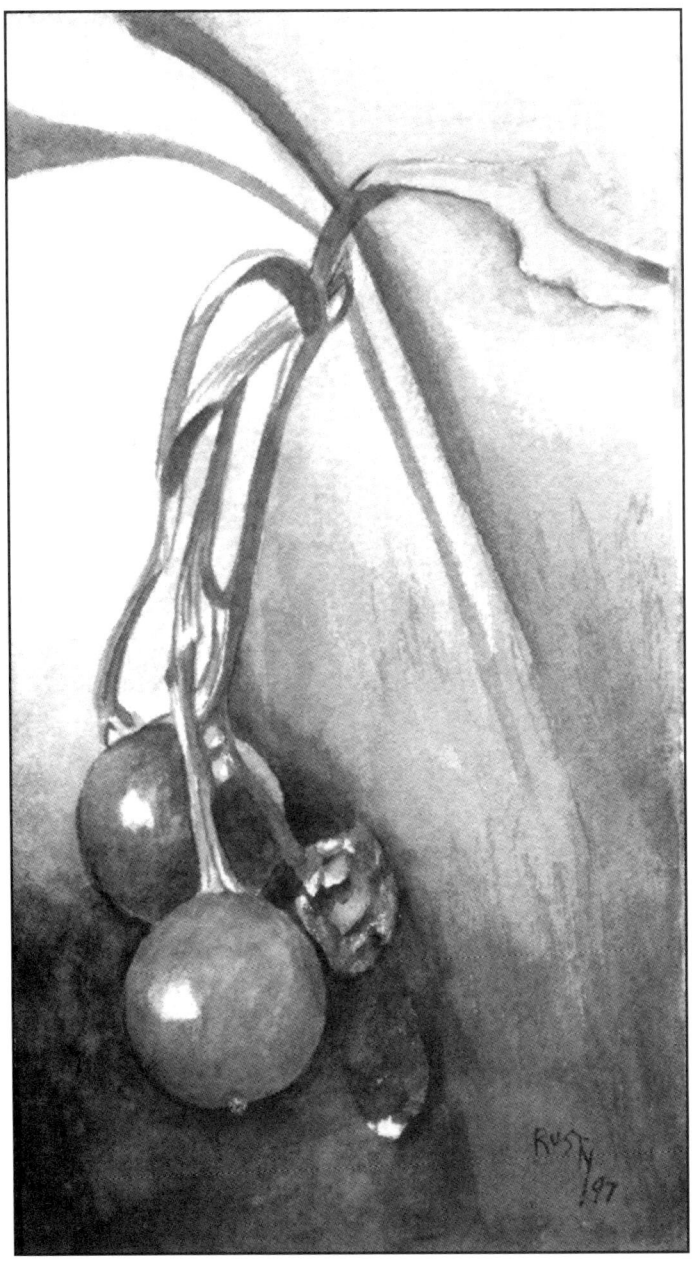

I

the house rises
the sound of the hammer goes deep

fall is in the air
and hunters return

I rise to the surface
move further and further into the dark

build   tear apart
are there no formulas

the voices of lost words   my light
will never hold their green eyes

II

the work of the past
is a thin sacrifice to man's dreams

my joints creak   your hands
are branches on the bark of my skin

apples like ideas fall
from the tree outside my window

signs by the road
scars of a river crossed

fire opened the buds before their time
some things are impossible to describe

III

a coat of nails covers your soul
my shirt is nailed to your door

your nylons are wrinkled
my sweater shows through your coat

if I talk of Portugal and black knights
it leads to poetry

varnish and warm wood   Your eyes are glass
my heart is stained walnut

we part   You hate roses and gather
onions of hope

even the soft deep of a sunset
is lost to some unknown

IV

forget the books
the roar of the brook goes deep

I leave what I know
the soil grows new life

rock grows nothing
death and decay give life

three generations out of the bush
how will I survive

only the cedars lean
to the rapids sound

V

the river overflows
nothing is left

with nowhere to go I sit
and clear my mind

there will be blood   the memory
of old scars   the opening of new

someone will learn that
they cannot take what is not theirs

clouds of mist   time
is not measured only by the growth of trees.

VI

the slow curve of the past
the opening of a flower after rain

the air cleans   the circle widens
there are messages I cannot understand

new ways to the same place   even while I sleep
there are poems   songs

the house grows   a nest of nerves
a flow of flowered pathways

already the book is settled with dust
the cover stained with a seasons jam

VII

facts folded like an accordian
in my mind

memories of struggling
to put feeling into words

I seize the sun
the moon cries

unsettled thoughts
waves on the shore

quit the struggle   no one stops the stream
or gather roses that fall to earth

VIII

cold wind howls
there is a garden I have never seen

move close   light candles
around the mattress on the floor

rise like a bear shaking shaking off a winter's sleep
listen to the metal on the furnace change shape

the rhythm   the rise
and fall of waves

leaving is like listening
to the flight of geese in fall

IX

graffiti covered walls   the band
hammers out songs of lost love

I smile and say little
not knowing what to expect

my head spins   the embers
rest among the ash

blackness at noon   the rattle
of half-ton trucks and seventies cars

sometimes words are taken for what they mean
not for the way they are said

X

the roots hang
my hands drip with blood

keep the fire   rise slowly
through the branches of trees

in winter I tunnel under snow
plunge into nothing

on the edge of the field
the living mix with the dead

there are boundaries
that are hard to cross

XI

I wander from room
to room   nowhere to go

guess I'll read a book
find some notes for my blue flute

you were born with the sun
I ride the moon

light must answer to the dark
sometimes

you find light in a metronome
I find it in patches of snow

XII

drive slow   in the cold
there are few tools for repairs

here   distance is measured in round figures
accidents are from animals crossing the road

I stumble through the light
adjust to the dark

gather the blood from the hearts of the fallen
bridge the gap between yesterday and today

the light fades   leaves crunch
like older paper under my feet

XIII

now   halfway through
I know I will return

inside there is a lake
that is cool and clear

does the sun shine without purpose
the wind blow without cause

too many questions   too much energy
the sum of everything before

perhaps I will end with nothing to remember
happy at the sight of my own blood

XIV

my legs shake
the lines unravel like yarn

there is no truth in a typewriter
no movement from one form to the next

fire flows   Words welded
chain complete

why climb so high   there is time
to add to what has not been said

and the cane made of birch
we all lean on something

wandering aimlessly I try to remember
my words damned by a feeling

XV

my poems   images reflected
from the cool water of a pond

I need something light that will dance
like a leaf or grasshopper in the wind

there is something about the coming together
of sounds around a pond at night

cranberries   red
against the snow

on damp days there is little
between the leaving and the arriving

XVI

the play of sunlight
and shadow on my door

pipes rattle   upstairs
someone reaches for light

mounds of earth
the ground   empty of life

I follow lines   a neighbor
pulls the stake from my heart

turn up the heat
tonight I need a warm coat

XVII

words   small births
of songs and need

under the lamp
ideas open   light enter

empty husks   the footprints
of those I follow but rarely see

a straight line   a curve
all things from the same place

the horse inside   the rider nameless
unknown even to himself

XVIII

the alder's
ice covered limbs

a coyote coiled up like an old spring
in the back of the truck

these cool unfinished fires

not neat and bare
like piled wood

but old carpet

snow   quietly falling   with the forest
cold and heavy on either side

XIX

when I write doors open   what's on the other side
darkness   a longing for more

the furniture   broken and worn
a value beyond the price paid

fish jump
words slide like ice

every day I get up
not knowing where to go

the noise inside settles
like dust on my thoughts

XX

the old apple tree defines its territory
forces itself towards the light

pull back the curtains
watch until I return

berries in blossom
somewhere someone remembers

I return from nowhere
fish belly their way upstream

the roots go back
the language of summer changes

XXI

the rapids spread over the pool as if covering
the entourage of a great king from the cold

rocks lie scattered on the bottom
like the speckled face of a laughing boy

I stare at the salmon who loll like dark logs
or rise slowly like flowers opening to to the light

prodigal's sons
they return to lay there eggs

their stomachs shrunk
to the size of a small black stone

XXII

snow curls like frozen waves
under the eves of my house

stars   burnt out centuries ago
sting with light

I stay low   snow swirls
wind sways the trees over my head

is there no place for refuge
no place for lost dreams

the clouds open
the cedars drip with joy

XXIII

blue herons walk the shore
of my pond for food

the hardwood stand
like the naked limbs of old women

when no one speaks
the birds listen

I look up   only emptiness
will I ever reach the end

tonight we will toss coins
at the moon

XXIV

on the edge of the field
the roots stretch the leaves into blossom

rain falls like the patter
of the feet of small animals

there is time to absorb the stillness
to reach through the dark

suddenly it's summer
the harvest returns

I think of full moons and laughter with you
folding chairs under the tree by the pond

II

XXV

the small stream   the fall rain
light gathers in the spaces between trees

breathe deep   there is no telling
how the spruce grow

wind moves   boards creak
there is warmth in an old blanket and knife

is that noise from a branch broken
by the foot of an old friend

quiet   the opening is not large
and the animals hear the smallest sounds

XXVI

light moves
through the hardwood

wind sways spruce
and fir

shadows lengthen across
snow covered fields

perhaps the roots of the fallen tree
were not deep enough

or the wind forced it
where it was not prepared to go

XXVII

for two days I drill for water
the walls cave in   I go nowhere in the sand

muscle and bone
is there no way to the light

roads unfurl
new ways to the past

I sink into substance
the water draws me like a lost chord

already I dream of dying
when I touch rock I will stop

XXVIII

I step into the soft edge
of the fall air

frost sparkles on the bark
of knarled trees

snow covers
the coarse ground

it feels like winter
I whisper

smiling
at the wonder

surreal
almost christian

XXIX

cedars arch triumphantly
over a road of dead leaves

flashlights
at the end of dark tunnels

under the lights cars
paw the street for food

drag clouds to the ground
that woman will not cover the cost of your fear

wandering like the needle of a seismograph
the dead rise like smoke from the ruins

XXX

the earth leans away
from the sun

last night   north wind
froze flesh

the salmon return hovering for position
and balance in the current

they wait for rain   memories
like small moons born inside months before

where the water cools spaces between rocks
hold the earth's gift to the sea

kingfishers and blue herons
are startled to flight

the sun burns the dew
from the grass

XXXI

dogs bark   far away
houses   cars

weeds rise on thin stalks
above the snow

boughs bend   hardwood
crack in the wind

I put my hand on the
rough bark of some spruce

the tops away with the sound
of the distant roar of a large plane

cold enters   the needles stiff like hair
on the back of a frightened deer

XXXII

scrape the frost from your dreams
the river flows two ways

the enemy wait on the shore
the fallen struggle in the current

there is no time to think about what might have been
about the way events work out

the colour green   the cross
what lies underneath

wait   read the footnotes crazy
with light and meaning

in those days a man lit
his tobacco with the sun

europe   a thin fog
lies on the land

XXXIII

why out the wrong way
fire will not burn without light

it's no good
that cheese factory went bankrupt years ago

I fall flat on my back   drunk
on the unholy push of heavy loads

now the big ones move in
our milk lost in the ditches of time

eyes on fire   nerves like steel
every current finds its way home

XXXIV

between then and now
a space I must find

eyes meet   the horizon
a straight line between points

miles away   a flower blooms
a brook fills with rain

the valve opens   the image flows
there is more than meets the eye

I feel for depth
look for colour

illusions   the distance stays
the apple falls

with age   lines bend
houses fall

around this
we build homes   lives

XXXV

this load needs rope
and a wagon with heavy springs

the load topples   the ground too steep
the wagon too full

pull the reins
whip the horse

light flows   wind blows
the needle moves

forget the cost   leave nothing
when I arrive I'll be home

XXXVI

I leave the truck by the main road   wash
the sleep of the town from my eyes

my mind absorbs the silence
the sun warms my back

northern pike cruise the currents
near the river's mouth to lay their eggs

I haul them gasping and squirming
onto the ice

that night   behind the ski-doo
Cy nurses wet feet in the toboggan

my fingers cold
inside damp gloves

XXXVII

dig deep
leave the familiar

the ground opens
roots bend

there is no need for names
the flowers grow wild by my door

earth cries
and cries

light for a time woven
into human form

XXXVIII

this time I'll learn
not to take too much

perhaps when we sleep but what good
is the world if we do not know

dampness and cold   pile wood

                                    by
the fire

                            read
by the silence of the clock

the lights go out
the radio's set for tomorrow

the truck windows fogged over with the stars
as bright as I remember them as a boy

XXXIX

a tent
of snow covered boughs

the illusion of depth
nothing stops the eye in its fall

quarter moon   trees
cradle of hills   campfire inside

dark clouds hover   what is above
unconnected to what is below

in the end   quiet travellers
we return to earth

XL

walking
on cushion soles

mulling the ink waters
of the past

the cloudy eyes
of saints

the mosquito glances
of women

the toast and jam smiles
of boys I never knew

there was a longing
in empty rooms and under stairs

where flames never saw
the winter sun

and guitars mooned
on the pastures of the old

XLI

the wind beats snow
against my house

threads hang from the coat of a man
filling the cracks in his home

last night a man with black hair
drank beer by the well house

he laughed through a crack in the door
I put more wood in the stove

I am warm leaning back
on the legs of his old chair

XLII (for John Thompson)

dark days   without fear
nothing lost or gained

I'm thinking of you John as ten flies
dance on the head of a spoon

reach bottom   then you'll know
the fear of living on your own

even the blue heron high on the limb of a spruce
waits for the lights to go out

houses   houses
when will I build my own

careful   when a woman lingers
by the iron anyone can fall

XLIII

alders   tamarack
deadwood blown over by the wind

in this field charred sticks
sent flames high into the air

I throw what I don't need
over the bank

                towards

the creek black and swollen
with last week's rain

the wind and the smell of freshly cut wood
a warmth even the cold cannot contain

XLIV

that morning he was too hard to
didn't want to be moved

the bed shaking each time
he gasped for air

slower   with more time
and distance between breaths

memories are thick and thoughts are dark
as we strut and stutter like geese

our arms limp and heavy
as old 2x4

XLV

words unspoken
gestures unseen

must I always feel
the pain in my stomach

if I could see the world
with one eye

do not bend the picture
I want to see for myself

my works as real as pumpkins
as solid as the concrete on my basement floor

XLVI

flowers bloom   too quickly
the tide turns again

a child falls through thin ice
over the current

a balance   the rustle
of leaves after a storm

there are dreams of light
paths through snow

the ice covered limbs of trees
touch the ground

XLVII

snow falls on the patge
where I write

hands reach deep
into earth

the houses are alone
and silent

the road has
a soft cover

where no one walks
the light from the moon fades

XLVIII

create or destroy
which will it be

damp air chills
is there no heat

leaves turn   time passes
flesh changes   the child grows

light for a time woven
into human form

A Selection of Titles in Print

96 Tears (in my jeans) (Vaughan)	0-921411-65-0	3.95
Best Lack All, The (Schmidt)	0-921411-37-5	12.95
Coils of the Yamuna (Weier)	0-921411-59-6	14.95
Cover Makes a Set (Blades)	0-919957-60-9	8.95
Cranmer (Hawkes)	0-921411-66-9	4.95
Crossroads Cant (Grace, Seabrook, Shafiq, Shin, Blades (ed.))	0-921411-48-0	13.95
Dark Seasons (Trakl; Skelton (trans.))	0-921411-22-7	10.95
for a cappuccino on Bloor (MacLean)	0-921411-74-X	13.95
Gift of Screws (Hannah)	0-921411-56-1	12.95
Heaven of Small Moments (Cooper)	0-921411-79-0	12.95
Herbarium of Souls (Tasić)	0-921411-72-3	14.95
I Hope It Don't Rain Tonight (Igloliorti)	0-921411-57-X	11.95
In the Dark—Poets & Publishing (Blades)	0-921411-62-6	9.95
Invisible Accordion, An (Footman (ed.))	0-921411-38-3	14.95
Lad from Brantford, A (Richards)	0-921411-25-1	11.95
Like Minds (Friesen)	0-941411-81-2	14.95
Longing At Least Is Constant (Payne)	0-921411-68-5	12.95
Notes on drowning (mclennan)	0-921411-75-8	13.95
Open 24 Hours (Burke; Reid; Niskala; Blades, mclennan)	0-921411-64-2	13.95
Poems from the Blue Horizon (mclennan)	0-921411-34-0	3.95
Poems for Little Cataraqui (Folsom)	0-921411-28-6	10.95
Milton Acorn Reading from *More Poems for People*. (C-45 cassette) (Acorn)	0-921411-63-4	9.95
Rant (Fowler-Ferguson)	0-921411-58-8	4.95
Rum River (Fraser)	0-921411-61-8	16.95
Seeing The World With One Eye (Gates)	0-921411-69-3	12.95
Speak! (Larwill; *et al*)	0-921411-45-6	13.95
St Valentine's Day (Footman)	0-921411-45-6	13.95
Strong Winds (Hyland (ed.))	0-921411-60-X	14.95
the bride of Inglish (Gousopoulos)	0-921411-70-7	12.95
There Are No Limits To How Far The Traveller Can Go (Gates)	0-921411-54-5	4.95
Under the Watchful Eye (Deahl)	0-921411-30-8	11.95

Your bookseller can order our books from **General Distribution Services:**, 325 Humber College Blvd, Toronto ON M3B 2T6, fax 416 213-1917 customer.service@ccmailgw.genpub.com : Toronto ph 416 213-1919; Ont./ Que. 1-800-387-0141; rest of Canada 1-800-387-0172; USA 1-800-805-1083. Sales representation by the **Literary Press Group of Canada**, ph 416-483-1321. Direct from the publisher, individual orders must be prepaid. Add $2 shipping for first book ($9.95 and up) and $1 per additional item. Canadian orders must add 7% GST/HST.

MARITIMES ARTS PROJECTS PRODUCTIONS
BOX 506 STN A
FREDERICTON NB E3B 5A6   Ph/fax: 506 454-5127
CANADA   E-mail: jblades@nbnet.nb.ca